NONFICTION

Essential Literary Genres

BY ALEXIS BURLING

Essential Library

An Imprint of Abdo Publishing | abdopublishing.com

ABDOPUBLISHING.COM

Published by Abdo Publishing, a division of ABDO, PO Box 398166, Minneapolis, Minnesota 55439.

Printed in the United States of America, North Mankato, Minnesota
082016
012017

THIS BOOK CONTAINS RECYCLED MATERIALS

Interior Photos: JMA/Star Max/Ipx/AP Images, 11; Hagit Berkovich/Shutterstock Images, 13; Graf/Getty Images, 15; Jeff Malet Photography/Newscom, 17, 45; AP Images, 18, 26; Margaret Bourke-White/The LIFE Picture Collection/Getty Images, 22–23; Alexander Gardner/Library of Congress, 35, 41; Silsbee, Case & Co./Library of Congress, 38; S. M. Fassett/Library of Congress, 43; Library of Congress, 49; Carol M. Highsmith/Library of Congress, 53; Science Source, 59; Bill Tiernan/Virginian-Pilot/AP Images, 61; Matthias Hiekel/Picture-Alliance/DPA/AP Images, 64; Daniel Boczarski/Getty Images, 67; SuperStock/Science Faction/Glow Images, 69; Morehouse School of Medicine/AP Images, 75; Mario Guti/iStockphoto, 80–81; Patrick Seeger/Picture-Alliance/DPA/AP Images, 85; Chiang Ying-ying/AP Images, 89; Liu Yilin Xinhua News Agency/Newscom, 90–91; Peter Bennett/Science Source, 97

Editor: Melissa York
Series Designer: Maggie Villaume

PUBLISHER'S CATALOGING-IN-PUBLICATION DATA

Names: Burling, Alexis, author.
Title: Nonfiction / by Alexis Burling.
Description: Minneapolis, MN : Abdo Publishing, 2017. | Series: Essential literary genres | Includes bibliographical references and index.
Identifiers: LCCN 2016945207 | ISBN 9781680783810 (lib. bdg.) | ISBN 9781680797343 (ebook)
Subjects: LCSH: Literature--Juvenile literature. | Literary form--Juvenile literature.
Classification: DDC 809--dc23
LC record available at http://lccn.loc.gov/2016945207

CONTENTS

1

INTRODUCTION TO LITERARY GENRES

Why do we read and write literature? Telling stories is an integral part of being human, a universal experience across history and cultures. Literature as we know it today is the written form of these stories and ideas. Writing allows authors to take their readers on a journey that crosses the boundaries of space and time. Literature allows us to understand the experiences of others and express experiences of our own.

What Is a Genre?

A genre is a specific category, or type, of literature. Broad genres of literature include nonfiction, poetry, drama, and fiction. Smaller groupings include subject-based genres such as mystery, science fiction, romance, or fantasy. Literature can also be classified by its audience, such as young adult (YA) or children's, or its format, such as a graphic novel or picture book.

What Are Literary Theory and Criticism?

Literary theory gives us tools to help decode a text. On one level, we can examine the words and phrases the author uses so we can interpret or debate his or her message. We can ask questions about how the book's structure creates an effect on the reader, and whether this is the effect the author intended. We can analyze symbolism or themes in a work. We can dive deeper by asking how a work either supports or challenges society and its values or traditions.

You can look at these questions using different criticisms, or schools of thought. Each type of criticism asks you to look at the work from a different perspective. Perhaps you want to examine what the work says about the writer's life or the time period in which the work was created. Biographical or historical criticism considers these questions. Or perhaps you are interested in what the work says about the role of women or the structure of society. Feminist or Marxist theories seek to answer those types of questions.

How Do You Apply Literary Criticism?

You write an analysis when you use a literary or critical approach to examine and question a work. The theory you choose is a lens through which you can view the work, or a springboard for asking questions about the work. Applying a theory helps you think critically. You are free to question the work and make an assertion about it. If you choose to examine a work using racial criticism, for example, you may ask questions about how the work challenges or upholds racial structures in society. Or you may ask how a character's race affects his or her identity or development throughout the work.

Forming a Thesis

Form your questions and find answers in the work or other related materials. Then you can create a thesis. The thesis is the key point in your analysis. It is your argument about the work based on the school of thought you are using. For example, if you want to approach a work using feminist criticism, you could write the following thesis: The character of Margy in Sissy Johnson's *Margy Sings the Blues* uses her songwriting to subvert traditional gender roles.

HOW TO MAKE A THESIS STATEMENT

In an analysis, a thesis statement typically appears at the end of the introductory paragraph. It is usually only one sentence long and states the author's main idea.

Providing Evidence

Once you have formed a thesis, you must provide evidence to support it. Evidence will usually take the form of examples and quotations from the work itself, often including dialogue from a character. You may wish to address what others have written about the work. Quotes from these individuals may help support your claim. If you find any quotes or examples that contradict your thesis, you will need to create an argument against them. For instance: Many critics claim Margy's actions uphold traditional gender roles, even if her songs went against them. However, the novel's resolution proves Margy had the power to change society through her music.

HOW TO SUPPORT A THESIS STATEMENT

An analysis should include several arguments that support the thesis's claim. An argument is one or two sentences long and is supported by evidence from the work being discussed. Organize the arguments into paragraphs. These paragraphs make up the body of the analysis.

Concluding the Essay

After you have written several arguments and included evidence to support them, finish the essay with a conclusion. The conclusion restates the ideas from the

HOW TO CONCLUDE AN ESSAY

Begin your conclusion with a recap of the thesis and a brief summary of the most important or strongest arguments. Leave readers with a final thought that puts the essay in a larger context or considers its wider implications.

thesis and summarizes some of the main points from the essay. The conclusion's final thought often considers additional implications for the essay or gives the reader something to ponder further.

In This Book

In this book, you will read summaries of works, each followed by an analysis. Critical thinking sections will give you a chance to consider other theses and questions about the work. Did you agree with the author's analysis? What other questions are raised by the thesis and its arguments? You can also see other directions the author could have pursued to analyze the work. Then, in the Analyze It section in the final pages of this book, you will have an opportunity to create your own analysis paper.

The Genres of Nonfiction

The book you are reading focuses on the genre of nonfiction. Nonfiction books are works that use collected research and factual information to explain a subject, event, or idea. Nonfiction also has many subgenres. In a biography, the author shares a written account of another person's life. A collection of essays groups a series of analytical or interpretive articles together regarding a range of topics or themes. A memoirist describes memories from his or her own life using the first person point of view. Historical texts often use maps, timelines, photographs, and other additional features to depict a period or event in history. Scientific texts are more technical; they explain biological, medical, ecological, or environmental concepts using clear, easy-to-understand language. As you'll see in this book, nonfiction books come in all shapes and sizes. Some draw from two or more subgenres, too. They can be expository, analytical, or even written in a narrative fashion, almost like a story.

LOOK FOR THE GUIDES

Throughout the chapters that analyze the works, thesis statements have been highlighted. The box next to the thesis helps explain what questions are being raised about the work. Supporting arguments have also been highlighted. The boxes next to the arguments help explain how these points support the thesis. The conclusions are also accompanied by explanatory boxes. Look for these guides throughout each analysis.

2

OVERVIEWS OF *ENCHANTED AIR* AND *BROWN GIRL DREAMING*

Margarita Engle is a Cuban-American poet and writer. She is the author of more than 15 novels and nonfiction books for teens, including *The Surrender Tree*, which received a Newbery Honor, and the Pura Belpré Author Award–winning *The Poet Slave of Cuba*. In 2015, she published the memoir-in-verse *Enchanted Air*, filled with poems about the first 14 years of her life.

Engle lives in California with her husband. But during her childhood, she traveled from Los Angeles, California, where she was born, to Cuba, where her ancestors planted their roots. As Engle explains in *Enchanted Air*, when her parents met on Valentine's Day

Engle won the PEN Literary Award for Young Adult Literature in 2014 for her book-in-verse *The Lightning Dreamer*.

in 1947, it was love at first sight. They saw each other from across a terrace in Trinidad—the city in Cuba where Engle's mother grew up.

At the time, Engle's mother was a local art student. Engle's American father had come to Trinidad after seeing photographs of the city in *National Geographic* magazine. Her mother and father didn't speak the same language. Their families and cultures were worlds apart. Yet the couple fell so deeply in love they got married. Four years later, in 1951, Margarita was born.

A Divided Self

When she was just a girl, Margarita took her first trip to Cuba. She was mesmerized by the "fairy-tale kingdom" full of wild parrots and exotic plants.[1] She fell in love with the "lush beauty" of her great-uncle's picturesque farm.[2] She adored the "peaceful hillsides" full of Zebu cows and galloping horses that roamed like "floating clouds / in the stormy / tropical sky."[3] When she and her family returned to California after the summer ended, Margarita was crushed. It felt as though "one of [her] two selves / [was] left behind" like a wave caught between two shores.[4]

Some streets in Trinidad, Cuba, are lined with colorful houses.

Margarita felt torn between two homes throughout her adolescence. She spoke two languages: English and Spanish. She also celebrated many different traditions: some from her Cuban relatives and others from her father's Jewish ancestors who immigrated to the United States to escape violence in Ukraine.

Still, Margarita did her best to adjust to life in Los Angeles. Her older sister, Mad, contracted polio but survived. The girls' father taught art and painted, while their mother, whom they called Mami, gardened and sewed. Margarita found comfort among the trees and animals in the woods. She did so well in school she skipped a couple of grades, and she read as many books as she could find.

Changes Ahead

One summer, the Engles vacationed in Mexico instead of going back to Trinidad. A revolution that erupted in Cuba in 1953 had grown steadily worse, and it was too unsafe to travel there. When Margarita's family returned home to Los Angeles, agents from the Federal Bureau of Investigation (FBI) showed up at the Engles' door to ask threatening questions about whether Margarita's mother was a Cuban communist and, therefore, an enemy of the US government.

In 1960, Mami decided it was worth the risk to visit her relatives. When she arrived first in Havana, Cuba, and then traveled to the farm in Trinidad with her daughters in tow, Cuba seemed like a changed country. Instead of vibrantly colored dresses and music in the streets, there were soldiers in drab uniforms carrying machine guns.

The threat of war was everywhere. Still, Margarita cherished running barefoot with her noisy Cuban cousins, riding horses, wandering among the towering palm trees, and listening to her great-grandmother's stories. Despite Mami's difficulty obtaining exit and entry visas—documents that permitted the family to leave Cuba and reenter the United States—no one wanted to leave. By the time the summer ended, Margarita was already dreaming of going back the following year.

Banned for Good

Margarita didn't return to her great-uncle's farm that next summer, or for many summers afterward. Instead, she stayed in California while tensions between the United States and Cuba escalated. On April 17, 1961, US-trained Cuban exiles attacked the island in the failed Bay of Pigs invasion. As a result, the United States cut

Cuban defenders repelled the attackers during the Bay of Pigs invasion.

off all diplomatic and trade relations with Cuba, and travel between the two countries was banned.

For Margarita, school had become uncomfortable because she was viewed as different from the other kids. The only real friends she had in sixth and seventh grade were books. She also started writing poetry and stories of her own.

In 1962, US spy planes photographed Russian nuclear weapons in Cuba, sparking the Cuban Missile Crisis between the two countries. From October 22 to 28, US Navy warships surrounded the island, and nuclear war seemed imminent. Air-raid drills happened regularly, with children in classrooms across the United States hiding under their desks in case of an atomic bomb attack.

The crisis was narrowly averted. By 1965, the anticommunist fever that arose in the United States during the Cuban Missile Crisis had been replaced by a new focus: the civil rights movement. People marched in the street, calling for equal rights for all races and later genders.

But Margarita's thoughts of Cuba never subsided. When she was 14 years old, the Engles took an extended trip across Europe. Experiencing so many cultural traditions reminded her that she could love many countries, not just two. Margarita hoped someday she could reunite with her other self in Cuba.

Brown Girl Dreaming: Two Homes

Jacqueline Woodson is an African-American poet and writer. She is the author of more than 30 books for children and teens, including three Newbery Honor Books: *Show Way*, *Feathers*, and *After Tupac & D Foster*. In 2014, she published the memoir-in-verse about her childhood, *Brown Girl Dreaming*, which won the National

Jacqueline Woodson spoke at the National Book Festival in 2012.

Book Award. A year later, she was appointed the Young People's Poet Laureate of the United States.

Jacqueline, or Jackie, was born on February 12, 1963, in Columbus, Ohio. Named after her father, Jack, she entered the world as the civil rights movement was beginning—a time when African Americans were "emancipated / but not free."[5] Ruby Bridges had recently become the first black student to desegregate an all-white school in Louisiana. Martin Luther King Jr. was planning the March on Washington, DC, calling for an end to prejudice in the country.

Six-year-old Ruby Bridges was escorted out of her all-white school in New Orleans, Louisiana, on November 14, 1960.

Jackie's parents fought often about whether to stay in a less bigoted Ohio or move back to Greenville, South Carolina, where Jackie's mother, MaryAnn, grew up. When Jackie was barely a year old, her parents divorced. Jack stayed in Ohio; MaryAnn took the children—Jackie, Odella, and Hope—to stay with their grandparents in Greenville.

Southern Living

The Woodsons encountered deep racism in the south, including segregated buses, ill-treatment in restaurants, and derogatory slurs muttered behind their backs. But Jackie's years in the mostly black Nicholtown neighborhood of Greenville were filled with happy experiences. She spent endless hours listening to her grandfather sing hymns and plant vegetables in the garden as her grandmother made fried chicken and served sweet tea in mason jars. On Saturday nights, her grandmother pulled out hot combs and hair grease and told stories about her childhood while straightening Jackie's and her sister's kinky curls.

Though Jackie's grandparents spent every minute they could with their grandchildren, they also worked hard to put enough food on the table. Jackie's grandfather was a foreman for a newspaper printing press, though he wasn't respected because he was black. Jackie's grandmother was employed part-time as a maid for wealthy white households. She went to worship regularly and made sure her grandchildren learned how to become Jehovah's Witnesses.

Jackie's grandparents loved taking care of the Woodson kids. But just when everyone had gotten used to the arrangement, Jackie's mother announced she was heading to New York City to find a new home. Around Jackie's fifth birthday, a letter arrived with shocking news. Not only had MaryAnn found an apartment, but she was also pregnant with Jackie's new baby brother, Roman.

New York Dreams

In between summer visits back to Greenville, Jackie's first few years in cold, gray New York were tough. The Woodsons moved frequently throughout Brooklyn and endured many tragedies. Jackie's Aunt Kay died in a falling accident. Her favorite Uncle Robert was arrested and sent to prison. Roman got lead poisoning from eating the paint on his bedroom walls. Jackie's beloved grandfather died, and her grandmother moved up north to live with her remaining family.

Yet throughout the hard times, the Woodsons rallied around each other and made the best of their circumstances. Odella read constantly and excelled in school. Hope concocted secret potions with his chemistry set and developed a gift for singing. And as for Jackie, she hung out on the stoop with her best friends, Maria and Diana—girls from Puerto Rico who also faced judgment and prejudice because of their ethnic background. As many of their classmates did, the trio championed the teachings of the Black Panthers, who demanded that nonwhites stand up for equal rights. Jackie marched in the streets and raised her fist in the air like Black Panther leader Angela Davis.

But the biggest change that happened during Jackie's childhood was internal. She had trouble reading and writing at first. But with practice and determination, she memorized words, let her imagination run wild, and began crafting poems and stories about gritty New York streets, memories of Greenville, and dreams of what her life could be. By the time she was a teenager, Jackie had figured out what she wanted to be: a writer.

3

A CHANGING SOCIETY

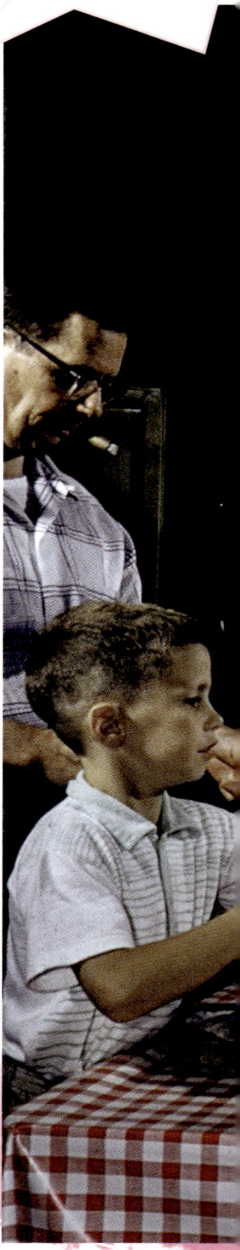

Historical criticism is a method of evaluating a work in terms of the historical context in which the piece was written. Historical critics might research social or cultural movements to determine how these events influence characters' actions. When considering memoirs, historical critics might also examine political events to see how they affected the life and psychological development of the author.

In *Enchanted Air*, Margarita Engle describes the first 14 years of her life, from summer trips to visit relatives in Cuba to her coming of age in Los Angeles. In *Brown Girl Dreaming*, Jacqueline Woodson recounts her

An African-American woman works in a white home in Greenville, South Carolina, in 1956, approximately a decade before Woodson lived there.

adolescent years in Greenville and in New York City. Engle and Woodson came of age during a period of great upheaval in the United States and abroad. Both of their memoirs take place primarily in the 1950s and 1960s. At the time, the United States was embroiled in the Cold War (1945–1991). This nonviolent conflict with the Union of Soviet Socialist Republics (USSR) and its allies, including Cuba, concerned the spread of communist influence in the democratic West. Back on the home front, Americans faced a different set of problems during the civil rights movement, mainly those involving race and gender. People marched in the streets, demanding desegregation and an end to racism, while women joined protests calling for the same economic and social rights as men. This constant turmoil affected Engle's and Woodson's lives in deeply significant ways. In *Enchanted Air* and *Brown Girl Dreaming*, the traumas the authors write about reflect the values of a US society not only dominated by prejudice and

THESIS STATEMENT

At the end of the first paragraph, the author states her thesis: "In *Enchanted Air* and *Brown Girl Dreaming*, the traumas the authors write about reflect the values of a US society not only dominated by prejudice and fear, but also teetering on the verge of change." The author will demonstrate how the United States' values during the 1950s and 1960s are echoed in the author's memoirs and show that the country was—and still is—ripe for improvement.

fear, but also teetering on the verge of change.

The struggles the Engles face throughout Margarita's childhood shed light on the United States' xenophobic outlook and hatred of communism during the Cold War years. From 1953 to 1959, Cuba was engulfed in a civil war. Communist revolutionary Fidel Castro and his rebel forces staged a successful coup against the US-backed Cuban president, Fulgencio Batista. Though Margarita is less than eight years old when the fighting in Cuba ends, she first learns at school in California what it means to be an outsider. Her teacher compares Americans in Cuba to Santa Claus, implying that Castro and his allies were ungrateful when they overthrew a dictator supported by the United States. This statement epitomizes the way many Americans shunned Cuban Americans during that time.

The mistreatment of the Engles doesn't stop there. The FBI visits the Engles' home to scrutinize Mami's

ARGUMENT ONE

Next, the author begins to support her thesis by presenting the first argument: "The struggles the Engles face throughout Margarita's childhood shed light on the United States' xenophobic outlook and hatred of communism during the Cold War years." She supports the thesis by providing examples of Americans' intolerance during Margarita's upbringing.

Fidel Castro would lead Cuba until he retired in 2008, succeeded by his brother Raúl.

possible connection to Cuban revolutionaries and investigate why Margarita's father took an art history class taught by a communist professor during World War II (1939–1945). Difficulties obtaining an entry visa from the US Department of Immigration nearly prevent Mami from leaving Cuba and reentering the United States in the summer of 1960. In 1962, after the Cuban Missile Crisis and all trade and travel between the United States and Cuba ceased, the Engles—along with many Cuban Americans—are banned from visiting their relatives in Cuba. Each of these events illustrates Americans' distrust of foreigners during the Cold War period, especially those from communist countries such as Cuba.

In contrast, whereas *Enchanted Air* addresses some of the political issues that influenced the United States' external outlook during the 1950s and 1960s, the ways in which Woodson and her family are discriminated against in *Brown Girl Dreaming* reflect many Americans' racist and sexist attitudes about each other during the same period. Looking back on her upbringing, Jackie describes a "country caught / between Black and White."[1] Part of her childhood takes place in Greenville, where her great-great grandparents worked as slaves in cotton fields. Though slavery was abolished in 1865 with the ratification of the Thirteenth Amendment, and Jackie spends much of her adolescence in a less-prejudiced Ohio and New York City, the reality she experiences is one in which blacks are "emancipated / but not free."[2]

ARGUMENT TWO

The author then presents the second argument by discussing the prejudiced mindset in the United States during Jackie's adolescence: "In contrast, whereas *Enchanted Air* addresses some of the political issues that influenced the United States' external outlook during the 1950s and 1960s, the ways in which Woodson and her family are discriminated against in *Brown Girl Dreaming* reflect many Americans' racist and sexist attitudes about each other during the same period."

In Greenville, Jackie's grandmother works as a maid cleaning rich white people's houses; known as daywork, it is one of the only jobs African-American women can get in the south at the time. Jackie's grandfather is employed as a foreman at a printing press, but his white colleagues often disregard his orders because he is black. Whenever the Woodsons travel by bus, they are forced to sit in the back or else face beatings by the police and white people looking at them "like [they're] dirt."[3] In restaurants, they're either ignored or placed by the kitchen where the African Americans, known derogatively as "coloreds," sit.

Though attitudes are more progressive in the north, the Woodsons—along with many ethnic groups at the time—are still forced to put up with unpleasant circumstances in New York City because of the color of their skin. Most of the Brooklyn neighborhoods Jackie's family lives in, especially Brownsville, are known for their poverty, gang violence, and crime. In Bushwick, the Woodson's apartment is poorly maintained, and Jackie's baby brother Roman suffers brain damage from eating the lead paint on his bedroom wall. Even when Jackie's best friend Maria visits her wealthy white friends in upstate New York, they automatically assume she's poor because her family is Puerto Rican.

Despite the prejudice Margarita, Jackie, and their respective families put up with in the course of two decades, *Enchanted Air* and *Brown Girl Dreaming* illustrate how the United States has slowly evolved into a more progressive, racially and culturally tolerant country. Though the Engles couldn't return to Cuba after the US government imposed a travel ban, Margarita writes in the author's note that she was able to go back to the country through a humanitarian-aid program in 1991 when the Cold War officially ended. Margarita's grandmother and mother also became US citizens. Evidence of positive change in the country is referenced throughout *Brown Girl Dreaming*, too. People of all backgrounds began moving to nonsegregated neighborhoods. Great numbers of people marched for equal rights for all races. African Americans began sitting at the front of the bus and at lunch counters where blacks weren't historically served. Black Panther Angela Davis inspired her followers to be

ARGUMENT THREE

The author finishes proving her thesis by providing a third argument, mainly that Americans' attitudes had gradually begun evolving in ways: "Despite the prejudice Margarita, Jackie, and their respective families put up with in the course of two decades, *Enchanted Air* and *Brown Girl Dreaming* illustrate how the United States has slowly evolved into a more progressive, racially and culturally tolerant country."

proud of their heritage. "This is the way brown people have to fight," Jackie's grandfather says. "You can't just put your fist up. You have to insist / on something / gently."[4]

In many ways, Engle's and Woodson's memoirs reflect much of the political and social unrest that occurred in the United States during the 1950s and 1960s. Fear of a global communist takeover, the threat of nuclear war, racial intolerance—each issue takes root in the books' pages. Yet by their memoirs' conclusions, both authors had come to terms with or moved beyond the struggles they faced during their childhoods. And they had also vowed to embrace their identities as writers of color in an increasingly connected and multicultural world. In turn, their stories might inspire future generations of readers to analyze their own places in history and take action on issues they deem important.

CONCLUSION

The final paragraph is the conclusion, in which the author summarizes the arguments made throughout the paper and restates her thesis using different language. In this essay, the conclusion reiterates the idea that *Enchanted Air* and *Brown Girl Dreaming* represent significant records of US history during a time of great political, social, and cultural upheaval.

THINKING CRITICALLY

Now it is your turn to assess the essay. Consider these questions:

1. The author's thesis statement claims *Enchanted Air* and *Brown Girl Dreaming* are memoirs about the politically charged 1950s and 1960s and are, therefore, important historical artifacts. Do you think the arguments effectively support this thesis? Why or why not?
2. In both memoirs, the authors describe feeling conflicted because they grew up in separate cultures. How did the events at the time in the United States shape this sensation? What examples can you pinpoint in the texts?
3. The author's conclusion upholds Engle and Woodson as role models for future generations of readers. Do you agree?

OTHER APPROACHES

The previous essay was only one way to critically analyze *Enchanted Air* and *Brown Girl Dreaming*. Another paper might use a religious approach, exploring the ways in which religion affected how Margarita Engle and Jacqueline Woodson interpret the world. A different option might look at the memoirs through a psychoanalytical lens, proving how each writer used words and language to rise above life's challenges.

Spiritual Guidance

Throughout her memoir, Woodson attests to the power of studying God's word. As a Jehovah's Witness, she finds peace and purpose by upholding the religion's beliefs: disavowing war, not celebrating holidays, and spreading her faith to others. In contrast, in *Enchanted Air* Engle looks to nature for spiritual fulfillment. The island palm trees, the manatees beneath the river in her great-uncle's farm, the woods outside her home in Los Angeles—each help Engle better understand her place in an increasingly complex and divided world. A thesis for an essay exploring these ideas might read: Woodson and Engle are both devout women, but their dissimilar religious and spiritual beliefs color their memoirs in different ways.

Writing as Therapy

Both writers admit to latching on to poetry at an early age. Engle uses words to describe the magical and vibrant world of Cuba, whereas Woodson depicts the cool breezes of South Carolina and the scratchiness of her beloved grandfather's voice using metaphors. Stringing words together into verse helped each author process and cope with milestone events, such as divorce, a grandparent's death, and war, during their childhood. A possible thesis statement arguing these ideas might be: Engle and Woodson came of age during tumultuous times in the United States, but because they learned how to use writing as a salve for life's frustrations and disappointments, they were able to mature into well-adjusted human beings.

4

AN OVERVIEW OF *CHASING LINCOLN'S KILLER*

It was March 4, 1865, and a noisy crowd gathered in front of the Capitol building in Washington, DC. They were waiting for President Abraham Lincoln to speak, marking the occasion of his second inauguration. As he rose from his chair and walked to the podium, the sun burst through the clouds overhead. "Fondly do we hope—fervently do we pray—that this mighty scourge of war may speedily pass away," he said."[1]

For four years, the United States had been entangled in a bloody civil war, with the Northern states fighting the Southern states. The two areas of the country disagreed about how the government should be run and, mainly, whether slavery should be legal. Northerners, who made up the Union army, thought the practice

Alexander Gardner captured the last portrait of President Lincoln on February 5, 1865.

was immoral and wanted to do away with it altogether. Southerners, called the Confederates, relied on slave labor to keep their plantations and businesses running. They were defending their right to keep slaves or they would withdraw from the Union and form a separate country.

On that March day, and every day before it since he was elected to office in 1860, Lincoln held firm in his belief that slavery should be outlawed. "I am naturally anti-slavery. If slavery is not wrong, nothing is wrong. I can not remember when I did not so think, and feel," he wrote to Albert G. Hodges, the editor of Kentucky newspaper the *Frankfort Commonwealth*, in 1864.[2] Yet the president was also determined to keep the United States together as one unified country and prevent the Southern states from seceding. Despite the fact that more than 600,000 lives had been lost in the war already, Lincoln was hoping for news of a win from the Union side.[3]

He didn't have long to wait. On April 3, 1865, the Union army captured Richmond, Virginia, the capital of the Confederacy. Six days later, Confederate general Robert E. Lee and his army surrendered to Union general Ulysses S. Grant at Appomattox Court

House. On April 11, President Lincoln gave a speech celebrating the end of the long war and victory for the North. In it, he called for limited citizenship and voting rights for African Americans. Everyone in the crowd was overjoyed. Everyone, that is, except one man: John Wilkes Booth. And thus begins James L. Swanson's book *Chasing Lincoln's Killer*, a thrilling true account of John Wilkes Booth's downturn and sudden demise.

A Plan for Revenge

Twenty-six-year-old Booth was a famous actor with fans throughout the country. He was also a Confederate sympathizer, and he was deeply angered by Lincoln's support of the Union cause. When Booth heard the president was planning to attend a performance on April 14 at Ford's Theatre, he vowed to seek revenge.

Just a few weeks earlier in mid-March, Booth and a crew of likeminded rebels had already plotted to take matters into their own hands. Their idea was to ambush Lincoln's carriage by gunpoint, kidnap the president on his way back to the Executive Mansion, and hold him hostage for the Confederacy, which could use the president to gain leverage in the war. But that plan failed. Lincoln's carriage never arrived. So Booth

John Wilkes Booth, photographed in December 1862

concocted a new scheme: killing Lincoln while the president was watching a play at Ford's Theatre. Booth's accomplices—Lewis Powell, David Herold, and George Atzerodt—were put in charge of killing Vice President Andrew Johnson and Secretary of State William H. Seward.

To prepare, Booth acquired his weapon of choice: a .44-caliber Derringer pistol. The gun could be fired once before it would have to be reloaded. If Booth didn't get the shot the first time around, he would use a knife.

On the evening of April 14, 1865, President Lincoln; his wife, Mary; and their guests Union major Henry Rathbone and his fiancée, Clara Harris, arrived late at Ford's Theatre. But Booth was ready. He talked his way past a servant who was guarding the door to the box where the group was sitting. He snuck in, aimed the gun at Lincoln's head, and pulled the trigger. When Major Rathbone jumped up to stop Booth from escaping, Booth stabbed the officer in the arm.

In his final act of the night, Booth leaped off the box ledge and onto the stage, injuring his leg. Undeterred, he raised the bloody knife into the air and bellowed, "The South is avenged!"[4] As Booth rushed out of the theater and into the night, Major Rathbone yelled from the balcony, "Will no one stop that man?" Harris shouted, "He has shot the president!"[5]

On the Run

Doctors tried to stem the blood from Lincoln's wound. But the president died the next morning at 7:22 a.m. in the back bedroom of a boardinghouse across the street from Ford's Theatre. Booth's coconspirators weren't as successful in their assassination attempts. Secretary of State Seward was brutally beaten in a bloody fight with Lewis Powell. But he survived after a police sergeant, George F. Robinson, and Seward's children attacked Powell. George Atzerodt, who was supposed to kill Vice President Johnson, was too afraid to carry out the plot.

Back at Ford's Theatre, audience member US Army Major Joseph Stewart chased Booth, but the actor got away on a horse. At approximately 10:30 p.m., Booth reached the Navy Yard Bridge that led from Washington into Maryland. He persuaded the soldiers stationed there, neither of whom had heard about the mayhem happening back in town, to let Booth cross. It was still dark when he reunited with Herold, who was supposed to be Powell's means of escape but had fled the scene of the crime. The two men stopped at a tavern in Surrattsville, Maryland, to pick up weapons and supplies that had been stashed there by the tavern owner, Mary Surratt. Then they rode south to Bryantown, Maryland, where Booth sought medical treatment for his broken leg from anti-Unionist Samuel A. Mudd. Mudd was a doctor who had signed on to participate in Booth's original plot to kidnap Lincoln.

Meanwhile, word had spread about the assassination, and a manhunt to find Booth was underway. Edwin M. Stanton, Lincoln's secretary of war, was in charge. Detectives and local police gathered clues and searched everywhere throughout Washington. Most leads turned up empty. One tip, from George Mudd, about two mysterious, grungy-looking strangers visiting his cousin Samuel's farm, was unfortunately ignored. Led by Lieutenant David Dana, troops from the Union army

David Herold went on the run with Booth.

established a command center in Bryantown to conduct a sweep of the Maryland countryside.

A Final Showdown

The next two weeks were filled with chaos. Lewis Powell and George Atzerodt had finally been captured in Washington. Both surrendered without a fight. President Lincoln was given a grand funeral in Washington on April 19. His body was sent to Springfield, Illinois, his hometown, to be buried. Booth and Herold were still on the loose.

On April 15, the two most wanted men in the country, with a $140,000 bounty on their heads, left Dr. Mudd's farm and traveled south. They got lost many times. They hid for days in a thicket and were almost discovered by Dana's army. Booth took the time to draft a letter to the *National Intelligencer* newspaper explaining his reasons for assassinating the president. Fully committed to their mission, the fugitives eventually made it across the Potomac River into Virginia on April 23. They had help from Confederate sympathizers Captain Samuel Cox and Thomas Jones, a Confederate Secret Service veteran who knew the rivers and woods of Maryland very well.

An ornate hearse carried Lincoln's body to his funeral.

But Booth and Herold's luck soon ran out. Thanks to a lucky tip, a new group of soldiers led by Sixteenth New York Cavalry Lieutenant Edward P. Doherty tracked the criminals to a barn in Port Conway, Virginia, on April 26. Trapped, Herold surrendered, but Booth refused. The troops set the barn on fire. Booth still didn't give himself up. Finally, a soldier named Boston Corbett shot Booth through one of the slats in the barn. Booth later died from his wound. After 12 days, the chase for Lincoln's killer was finally over. On July 7, 1865, the rest of Booth's accomplices—David Herold, George Atzerodt, Lewis Powell, and Mary Surratt—were hanged.

5

LITERARY ELEMENTS IN NARRATIVE NONFICTION

Nonfiction is often thought of as textbooks, news articles, or long-form journalism pieces, which contain information that is clearly laid out in a sequential manner. But there is also a subgenre of nonfiction in which facts are presented in a narrative style using the same type of literary techniques used in novels or short stories, such as character development and dialogue. It's called narrative or creative nonfiction. When analyzing narrative nonfiction, paying attention to the work's writing style—specifically the author's use of literary techniques—is essential to interpreting its overall meaning.

Author James L. Swanson adapted *Chasing Lincoln's Killer* for a younger audience from his adult-audience book *Manhunt*.

When author James L. Swanson sat down to write a book about President Abraham Lincoln's assassination for young readers, he had pored over mountains of original documents. But something was missing. Swanson needed a way to turn the research he had done into a finished product that might be interesting—even thrilling—to readers.

The completed book, *Chasing Lincoln's Killer*, is an excellent example of why narrative nonfiction is an effective way to teach and learn history. It takes the true events leading up to and succeeding the murder and weaves them into a story full of suspenseful moments. Swanson's use of literary devices—rising and falling action, character development, and a limited third-person point of view—helps readers gain a more comprehensive understanding of Lincoln's assassination and its larger effect on history.

THESIS STATEMENT

The author begins with a short explanation of narrative nonfiction as it relates to *Chasing Lincoln's Killer*. Then at the end of the third paragraph, she states her thesis: "Swanson's use of literary devices—rising and falling action, character development, and a limited third-person point of view—helps readers gain a more comprehensive understanding of Lincoln's assassination and its larger effect on history." The author will prove why *Chasing Lincoln's Killer* can be classified as narrative nonfiction and how the literary techniques Swanson uses help inform the work.

Though history students might already be aware of the basic facts surrounding Lincoln's death, Swanson's method of transforming the facts into a story with rising and falling action, a pulse-raising climax, and a denouement not only advances the plot, but also gives readers a gripping sense of how the events actually played out. Swanson sets up the premise in the introduction and the first few chapters: John Wilkes Booth and his gang of thugs are angered by the South's loss in the American Civil War (1861–1865). They tried to kidnap President Lincoln as an incentive for the Confederates to keep fighting but failed. So Booth comes up with a new plan to achieve the same purpose: murder the heads of state.

To keep readers on the edge of their seats, Swanson then employs not just one story arc, but two. The first—the assassination attempts on Lincoln, Vice

ARGUMENT ONE

Next, the author begins to support her thesis by presenting the first argument. "Though history students might already be aware of the basic facts surrounding Lincoln's death, Swanson's method of transforming the facts into a story with rising and falling action, a pulse-raising climax, and a denouement not only advances the plot, but also gives readers a gripping sense of how the events actually played out." The author will show why reading about history can be more interesting and thrilling when facts are presented like a story

President Johnson, and Secretary of State Seward—is filled with unexpected turns. In the book's rising action, Booth and Lewis Powell are confident they can carry out their evil deeds, but they are met with a few surprises. Booth wasn't expecting a servant to be outside Lincoln's theater box and didn't foresee injuring his leg in his jump to the stage. Powell was caught off guard when his gun misfired while he was attacking Seward. By including these twists, Swanson proves just how difficult the multilayered scheme really was to pull off.

After Lincoln's murder and Seward's assault, the action falls slightly with Lincoln's funeral, until it rises again at a rapid pace as Booth and David Herold go on the run to escape punishment. By this time in the narrative, Swanson has readers hooked and piles on near misses to keep the momentum going. For example, Booth and Herold get lost multiple times, and Lieutenant Dana decides not to follow up on George Mudd's tip about "two suspicious strangers [who] visited his cousin's farm seeking medical attention."[1] The climax, with the shootout between Booth and the Yankee cavalry at the Garrett's barn, is infused with so much tension readers might find themselves holding their breath until it's over. A denouement—the trial and

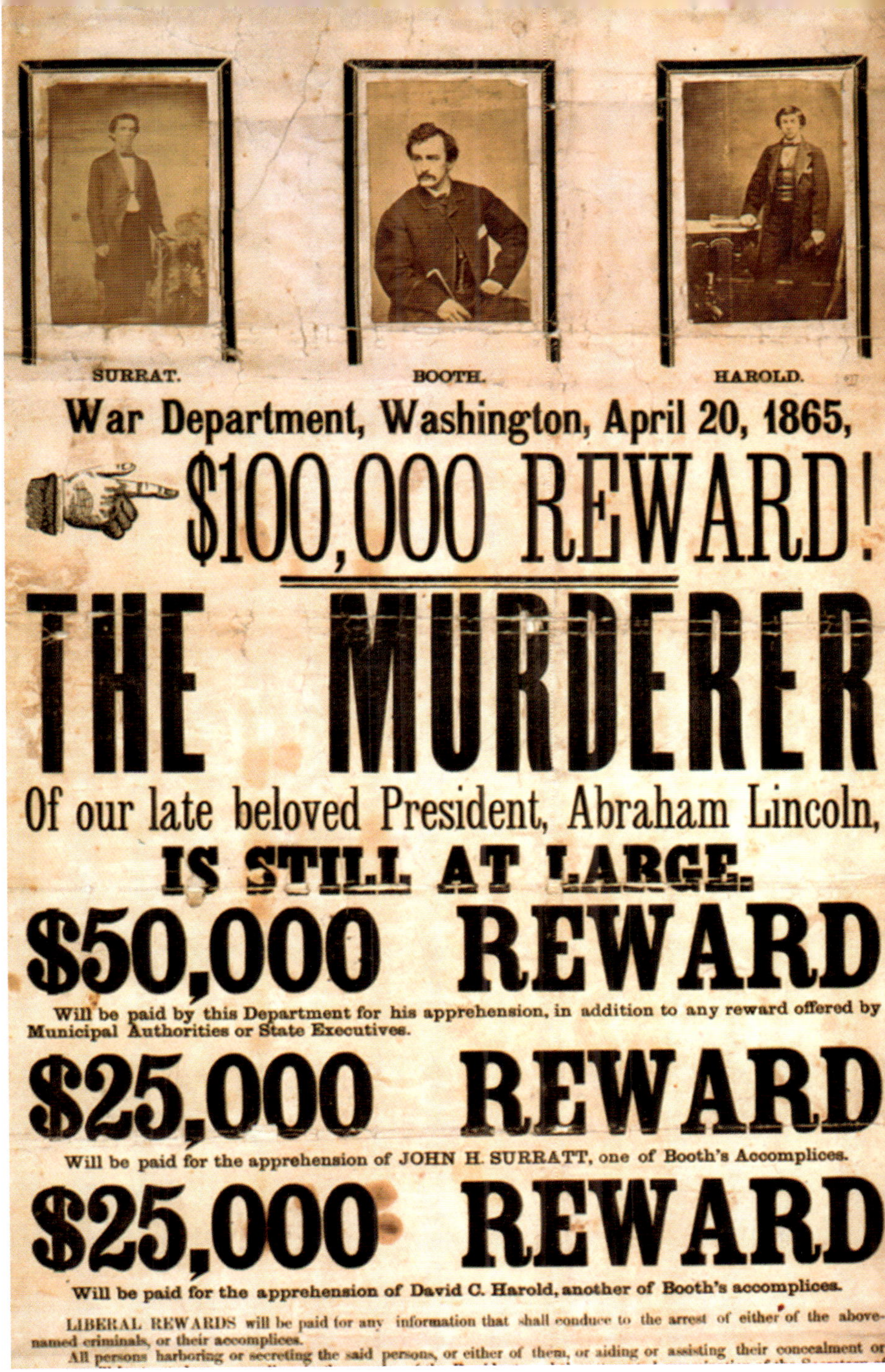
SURRAT. BOOTH. HAROLD.

War Department, Washington, April 20, 1865,

$100,000 REWARD!

THE MURDERER

Of our late beloved President, Abraham Lincoln,

IS STILL AT LARGE.

$50,000 REWARD

Will be paid by this Department for his apprehension, in addition to any reward offered by Municipal Authorities or State Executives.

$25,000 REWARD

Will be paid for the apprehension of JOHN H. SURRATT, one of Booth's Accomplices.

$25,000 REWARD

Will be paid for the apprehension of David C. Harold, another of Booth's accomplices.

LIBERAL REWARDS will be paid for any information that shall conduce to the arrest of either of the above-named criminals, or their accomplices.

All persons harboring or secreting the said persons, or either of them, or aiding or assisting their concealment or

A broadside advertised the reward for the capture of Lincoln's assassin and accomplices.

the book's epilogue that follows—serves as a satisfying conclusion and a vehicle for telling readers what happened to Booth's accomplices.

ARGUMENT TWO

The author then presents the second argument by discussing how treating Booth like a character—and discussing his motives, strengths, and weaknesses—adds depth to the story: "In addition, Swanson portrays the people involved as flawed individuals with complicated motives so readers will understand they were real people, not just one-dimensional characters."

In addition, Swanson portrays the people involved as flawed individuals with complicated motives so readers will understand they were real people, not just one-dimensional characters. The best example of this idea is Swanson's portrayal of Booth. Though readers recognize his name as a notorious killer, Booth wasn't an entirely evil person. Before his name was linked to Lincoln's in history, Booth was a highly respected man. The 26-year-old was an "extremely talented," good-looking actor from a show business family. He was "instantly recognizable to thousands of fans in both the North and South."[2] Booth was so well liked he could have gotten a one-on-one meeting with the president without raising any suspicion. By including these details, Swanson shows Booth had many good qualities in addition to the character flaws for which he was later known.

Swanson also demonstrates Booth's humanity by explaining the actor's motives for carrying out such a terrible mission. At the time, the North had just defeated the South and the Confederates were furious. They didn't want to give up their slaves, nor did they want African Americans to obtain important rights such as voting. Booth, like many Southerners, saw Lincoln's efforts as a betrayal to the Confederate beliefs and way of life. In Booth's eyes, it was his heroic duty to do whatever it took to fight for the Confederate cause, even if it meant murdering the president. He was so sure of this notion that he was surprised to find newspapers had labeled him a villain and wrote a letter to history explaining how and why he committed the crime.

Plus, in more ways than one, Booth didn't act alone. His extreme actions were abominable, but they didn't stem from a unique or mentally unstable way of thinking. Booth succeeded because he recruited accomplices who also wanted to get the pro-Union president out of power. A true antihero, Booth was an imperfect character who was bold enough to carry out the will of many.

ARGUMENT THREE

The author finishes proving her thesis by providing a third argument that demonstrates how a third-person point of view keeps readers engaged in the narrative of Lincoln's murder: "Finally, Swanson's use of a limited third-person point of view allows readers to take a more active role in the story and gain a more comprehensive grasp of history."

Finally, Swanson's use of a limited third-person point of view allows readers to take a more active role in the story and gain a more comprehensive grasp of history. In limited third-person point of view, the author knows only some of the characters' thoughts and feelings and relates all action using pronouns such as she or he. The real John Wilkes Booth didn't leave any explanation behind as to why he used a Derringer instead of a revolver to kill Lincoln. "Booth was a thrill seeker, so perhaps he wanted to increase his excitement by risking the use of a one-shot pistol. Or did he believe it more heroic, more honorable—even more gentlemanly—to take his prey with a single bullet?" Swanson writes in chapter 1.[3] By posing this question to readers, Swanson opens up history to interpretation. If Booth had chosen a revolver instead, maybe more people would have died that night.

Further, in using words and phrases such as *probably*, *would have*, and *seemed to* throughout the book, Swanson

The pistol Booth used to shoot Lincoln is now kept at the Ford's Theatre National Historic Site

shows he is not an omniscient narrator. This further demonstrates how some aspects of history will always remain a mystery. For example, there is no way to know for sure what Booth was actually thinking when he pulled the trigger. There is no way to know what would have happened next if Powell had succeeded in killing Secretary of State Seward. But by writing scenes in the most likely way they would have transpired, Swanson gives readers the facts and also allows them to use their imaginations to fill in the details moment by moment.

The murder of President Lincoln was one of history's most heinous acts. According to many experts, John Wilkes Booth was a monster who deserved to be shot for what he did. But as Swanson demonstrates in *Chasing Lincoln's Killer*, Booth had his reasons. And although those of us on this side of history might not agree with their beliefs, the Confederates who wanted to secede from the Union also had reasons for their actions. In the end, history is a complicated matter. It is because of Swanson's knack for thorough, thrilling storytelling that we are able to gain an informative glimpse of what most likely transpired during those particular moments.

CONCLUSION

The final paragraph is the conclusion, in which the author summarizes the arguments made throughout the paper and restates her thesis using different language. In this essay, the conclusion reiterates the idea that much of *Chasing Lincoln's Killer*'s success is due to Swanson's use of literary devices to inspire readers to get more involved in one of the most complicated and terrifying periods in US history.

THINKING CRITICALLY

Now it is your turn to assess the essay. Consider these questions:

1. The author's thesis statement claims literary devices such as character development and a third-person point of view inspire a more interactive and stimulating reading experience. Do you think the arguments effectively support this thesis? Why or why not?
2. The author uses John Wilkes Booth as an example of a three-dimensional character in *Chasing Lincoln's Killer*. Are there other characters in the book that might serve as good examples? How does understanding their motives help you understand the events covered in the book?
3. A conclusion should summarize the supporting arguments and partially restate the thesis. Does the conclusion presented in this paper do a good job of summing up the essay? How could it be improved?

OTHER APPROACHES

The previous essay was only one way to critically analyze *Chasing Lincoln's Killer*. Another paper might use a political approach, exploring how the political atmosphere of the time shaped each character's actions and reactions. Another option might look at the book through a structural lens, discussing how additional textual elements create a more informed whole.

A Political Approach

President Lincoln was killed partly because he advocated for the end of slavery and signed the Emancipation Proclamation in 1863, freeing many slaves. Although most Southerners might not have officially supported murdering the president, they were certainly willing to fight in the Civil War and help Booth do the dirty work to keep the practice of slavery alive. A thesis for an essay exploring these ideas might read: Though it was an act of one disgruntled man and his small band of henchmen, President Lincoln's assassination can be viewed as an action supported by a larger portion of society in response to what many Confederates believed to be the negative outcome of the Civil War.

Structural Guidance

Chasing Lincoln's Killer reads like an edge-of-your-seat mystery novel. But it also has elements seen in typical textbooks. An introduction explains the background of the Civil War. An author's note sheds light on why the author was inspired to write a book based on Lincoln's life and assassination. Numerous reproductions of newspaper clippings, photographs, legal documents, and maps both indicate authenticity and provide additional information about the subject. Each of these components contributes to the overall structure—and broader meaning—of Swanson's work. A possible thesis statement arguing these ideas might be: *Chasing Lincoln's Killer* is a compelling historical thriller augmented by a structure that compliments and informs the narrative.

6

AN OVERVIEW OF *THE IMMORTAL LIFE OF HENRIETTA LACKS*

Sixteen-year-old Rebecca Skloot was sitting in biology class in 1988 when something her professor said made Skloot snap to attention. He was describing a set of cancerous cells known as "HeLa" and called them "one of the most important things that happened to medicine in the last hundred years."[1] Unlike other human cells, which die a few weeks after they are removed from the body, HeLa cells thrive and reproduce at a rapid rate. According to one scientist, from the time they were taken from a tumor on a patient's cervix in 1951 to 1988, the HeLa cells replicated trillions of times—enough to make at least three loops around the earth.

Henrietta Lacks unknowingly gave the HeLa cells to science when she died in 1951.

HeLa are the world's first set of immortal human cells to be grown in a laboratory. They are directly linked to dozens of significant scientific breakthroughs, including the polio vaccine, genetic cloning, and the development of drugs that treat leukemia and Parkinson's disease. But when Skloot tried to learn more about the patient to whom the first HeLa cells belonged, she could find out only two pieces of information from her professor. The patient's name was Henrietta Lacks and she was black. It was then that Skloot came up with the idea for her first book, *The Immortal Life of Henrietta Lacks*: the true story of how HeLa came to be.

HeLa: The Woman

Henrietta Lacks was born Loretta Pleasant on August 1, 1920, in Roanoke, Virginia. She lived in a run-down shack near the railroad tracks with her parents and eight older siblings. When her mother died in childbirth four years later, the Pleasant children were split up among relatives. Henrietta went to stay with her grandfather, Tommy, and nine-year-old cousin, David (Day), two hours away in Clover, Virginia. They lived in a four-room log cabin adjacent to a tobacco farm that didn't have indoor plumbing or electricity.

Henrietta grew up in this log house in Clover, Virginia

When they weren't attending the "colored" school in their small town, Henrietta and Day picked tobacco and accompanied their grandfather to the market in South Boston, Virginia. She and Day became quite close and despite being cousins had two children together—the first when Henrietta was 14 years old and the second, a girl with a mental disability named Elsie, when Henrietta was 18 years old. The cousins married on April 10, 1941, when Henrietta was 20 and Day was 25. A year later, they moved to Turner Station, 20 miles (30 km) outside of Baltimore, Maryland.

Henrietta's life in Turner Station was filled with singing, dancing with her cousin Sadie, working around the house, and making occasional trips to visit Elsie, who had been committed to Crownsville State Hospital. Though Day earned a reputation for seeing other women around town, Henrietta looked past his cheating because she wanted to keep the family together. She was 30 and had given birth to another daughter named Deborah and a son named Joe. But on January 29, 1951, Henrietta felt a "knot on [her] womb."[2] Most clinics catered specifically to whites at that time, so Day drove her to the sole "colored only" public ward in the area, at Johns Hopkins Hospital. What she found out was very distressing: there was a cancerous tumor on her cervix. The diagnosis was stage 1, the earliest, least aggressive stage. But the cancer was still invasive and Henrietta needed to be treated immediately.

For the next few months, Henrietta underwent a series of procedures to combat the cancer. Gynecologist Howard Jones and his boss Richard Wesley TeLinde, one of the top cervical cancer experts in the country, gave Henrietta doses of radium. The treatment was so potent it could kill cancer cells, but it could also burn the skin off a patient's arm. Though the tumor shrank initially, it reappeared and spread to her uterus, urethra, and both kidneys. On August 8, one week after her thirty-first birthday, Henrietta checked herself into Johns Hopkins for good. The cancer had spread throughout her body. She died on October 4, 1951, at 12:15 a.m.

HeLa: The Controversy

Henrietta Lacks's death would have gone unnoticed by the world except for one thing: her surgeon, Dr. Lawrence Wharton Jr., had taken two tissue samples from her cervix before she died, one of healthy cells and one of cancerous cells. He gave them to Dr. George Gey, the head of tissue culture and research at Johns Hopkins, who had them divided into test tubes. Gey observed that Henrietta's cancerous cells were growing at an astonishing speed—nearly 20 times faster than normal cells grow. In fact, the cells reproduced so quickly they doubled in quantity every 24 hours.[3] Gey's assistant, Mary Kubicek, named the cells HeLa, after the first two letters of Henrietta's first and last name.

After this miraculous medical breakthrough, Gey realized his investigation had only just begun. He started giving HeLa cells away to any scientists who might want to use them for cancer research. Those scientists then gave them to other scientists, who used them to test drugs and research cures for major illnesses, such as chicken pox and measles. Before long, HeLa cells were commonplace in laboratories around the world.

After Henrietta died, Gey conducted an autopsy and took more samples from many of her organs. By 1953, there was so much scientific interest in HeLa cells that a factory was built for the sole purpose of reproducing and housing HeLa cells to help stop polio. The Tuskegee Institute created a distribution center that produced 20,000 tubes that housed 6 trillion cells each week.[4] The Microbiological Association then built the first for-profit cell delivery center. Despite the discovery in 1966 that HeLa cells could contaminate other cell cultures by traveling on scientists' hands or through

The Lacks family has received no money from the scientific use of HeLa cells. But since 2013 they have had a say in who is allowed to use the cells' genetic information for research.

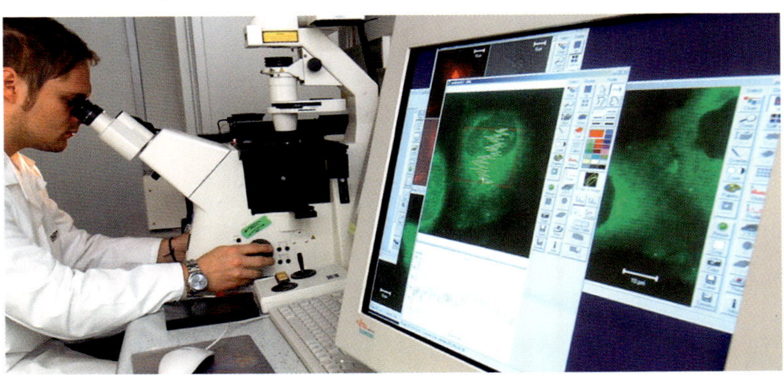

the air, the effect of HeLa on medicine was clear. It had ballooned into a multibillion-dollar industry.

There was only one problem: no one had asked Henrietta's permission to take those first samples. Gey believed it was his right to use the cells because Henrietta's treatment in the public ward was initially free. After she died, no one told her relatives about the research being done using her cells. When members of the media approached Gey in hopes of writing an article about the HeLa phenomenon, he told them to use a fake name when discussing the original patient. Thus, although pharmaceutical companies, scientists, and doctors were busy making a profit off of HeLa, Henrietta's five children and their offspring spent the next 20 years struggling from lack of money and medical insurance. "Them doctors never said nuthin about keepin [Henrietta] alive in no tubes or growin no cells," remembers Day Lacks. "All they told me was they wanted to do [an autopsy] see if they could help my children."[5]

Skloot Steps In

By the time Rebecca Skloot, then age 27, approached Henrietta's daughter Deborah in 1999 about writing a book about her mother, the Lackses already had weathered their share of disappointments. Elsie died alone when she was 15 at Crownsville State Hospital in 1955. All of the surviving Lacks children were still desperately poor. Deborah had entered into an abusive marriage that ended in divorce and was on her second marriage, while Joe, who changed his name to Zakariyya, spent 15 years in jail for murder.

Deborah and her brothers had also spent the last 20 years running from scientists and reporters who refused to tell the Lackses the truth about how Henrietta died and what was being done with her cells. One crook, who called himself Dr. Sir Lord Keenan Kester Cofield, said he was Deborah's husband's long-lost relative and a lawyer. He claimed he could help the Lackses sue Johns Hopkins. Cofield turned out to be a fraud with more than 150 fake cases under his belt. The deception ratcheted up Deborah's already heightened anxiety.

Understandably, the Lackses were initially skeptical about Skloot's motives. But with perseverance and dozens of phone calls in the course of a year, Skloot finally convinced the family to cooperate. For the next ten years, she crisscrossed the country conducting

Skloot wanted to learn more about Henrietta and tell her story.

hundreds of interviews for what would become *The Immortal Life of Henrietta Lacks*, often with an increasingly resourceful Deborah at her side. Skloot also did everything she could to help the Lackses gain access to information about their mother and her legacy. After her book was published in 2010, she donated part of its proceeds to the Lackses. She also set up the Henrietta Lacks Foundation to provide financial assistance to people like Henrietta who helped advance scientific research without benefiting from their contributions. Because of Skloot's efforts, the world finally knows the true story of the woman behind the most famous cells in history.

7

DISCRIMINATION IN MEDICINE

Critical race theory examines the way race is treated in a piece of literature. It focuses on the relationship between race and social class, economic status, and power. Racial critics might research historic changes or events, such as the abolition of slavery following the Civil War, the desegregation of schools during the 1950s and 1960s, or the civil rights movement during the 1950s through the 1970s, to explore how these milestones are reflected in a fictional work. Or, in the case of nonfiction, a critical race theorist might analyze examples from the text to form conclusions about how racism affected society at the time the work was written.

When Skloot started researching the life of Henrietta Lacks, she was surprised to find little to no information about the topic except the occasional photo of Henrietta

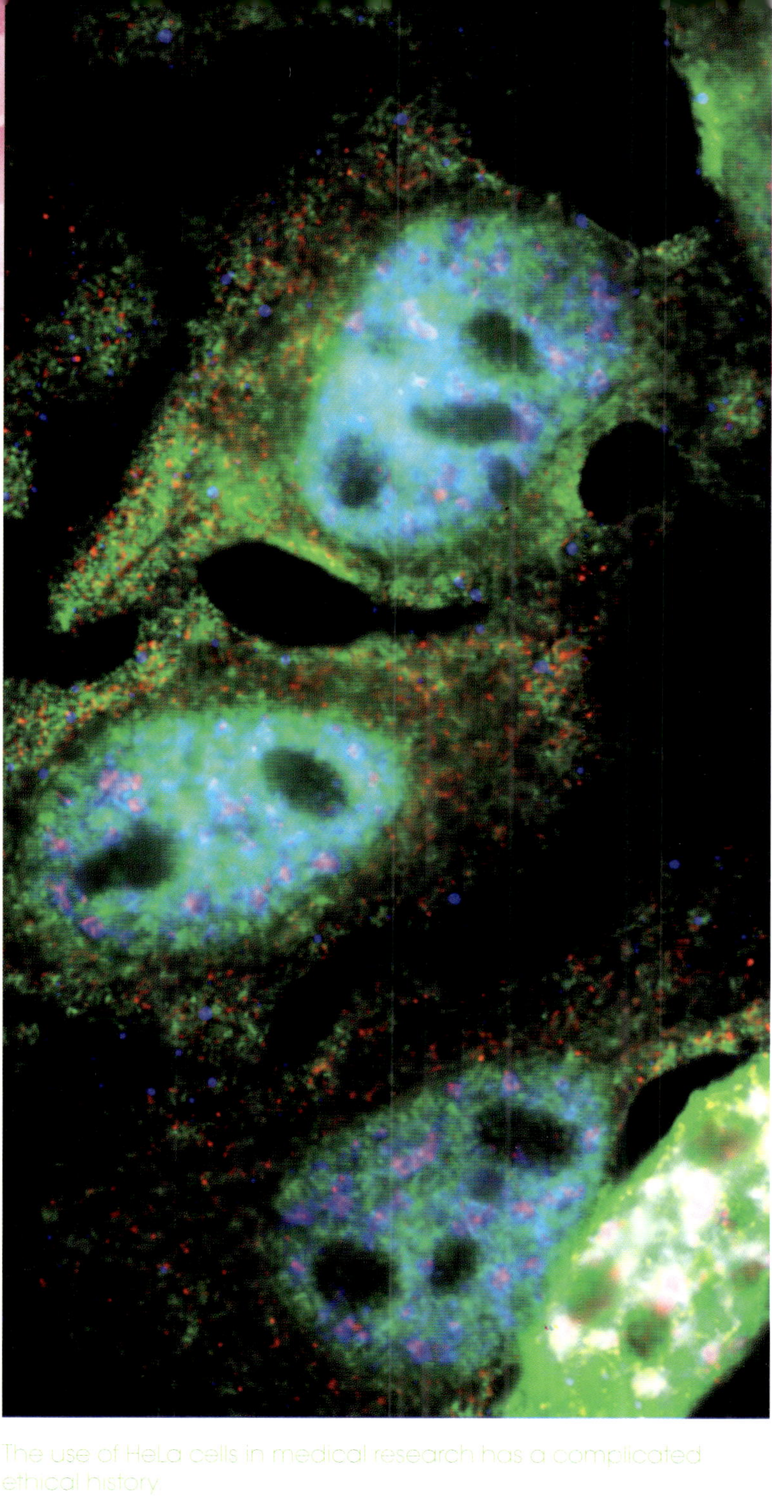

The use of HeLa cells in medical research has a complicated ethical history.

with an incorrect name attached. But in 1951, when the first HeLa cells were discovered, it wasn't that unusual for a black woman to be ignored—even a woman responsible for a major scientific breakthrough. At the time, the south enforced Jim Crow laws, a series of local and state ordinances that mandated racial segregation in southern states. If you were black and poor in the south during the 1950s, you were considered a second-class citizen.

Nearly 60 years later, Skloot attempted to change that perception and still faced significant pushback. She was accused of conspiracy. She was even pushed into a wall during an interview. But after nearly ten years of research, she completed the project and achieved an important victory in the fight against racism. In *The Immortal Life of Henrietta Lacks*, Skloot both sheds light on and upends racial stereotypes by highlighting decades of racist practices in the white-dominated medical industry and

THESIS STATEMENT

The author states her thesis: "In *The Immortal Life of Henrietta Lacks*, Skloot both sheds light on and upends racial stereotypes by highlighting decades of racist practices in the white-dominated medical industry and empowering the poor, black family who was in the dark for decades about its mother's important legacy." The author will discuss how race informs the events in the book.

empowering the poor, black family who was in the dark for decades about its mother's important legacy.

Although *The Immortal Life of Henrietta Lacks* is first and foremost a biography of the African-American woman whose cancerous cells singlehandedly changed the course of medicine, it is also a record of racist behavior in the scientific community during the 1900s. As Skloot shows in the text, it was difficult for many African Americans to get medical treatment in the 1950s. Most hospitals and clinics were reserved for middle- to upper-class whites. If African Americans showed up in a white-only emergency room, they'd likely be thrown out, "even if it meant they might die in the parking lot."[1]

ARGUMENT ONE

Next, the author starts supporting her thesis by presenting the first argument: "Although *The Immortal Life of Henrietta Lacks* is first and foremost a biography of the African-American woman whose cancerous cells singlehandedly changed the course of medicine, it is also a record of racist behavior in the scientific community during the 1900s." The author will draw conclusions about how the events in the book reflect larger racist practices in society.

Some hospitals, such as Johns Hopkins, did treat African Americans like Henrietta in their segregated wards. But Skloot makes the crucial connection that this decision to provide medical care wasn't solely out of goodwill. “Many scientists believed that since patients were treated for free in the public wards, it was fair to use them as research subjects as a form of payment,” she writes.[2] To further prove her point that African Americans have long been used as experiments in medical experiments, Skloot provides more examples from history. In the 1800s, doctors performed surgical procedures on slaves for practice, often without anesthesia. In the 1930s, the US Department of Public Health researchers at the Tuskegee Institute conducted research on black people with syphilis to observe how the disease progressed and killed, but they withheld a cure even after the drug’s discovery. As recently as the late 1990s, Johns Hopkins conducted a study in which homes with elevated lead levels were rented out to African-American families. When one child developed lead poisoning and Johns Hopkins failed to alert the parents, the hospital was sued. In each of these cases, poor, uneducated African Americans were used or abused because they were perceived by doctors to be dispensable.

The mere existence of *The Immortal Life of Henrietta Lacks* also demonstrates how prejudice both inhibited Skloot’s progress as a journalist and worked in her favor. After 20 years of dealing with tight-lipped doctors, crooks such as Dr. Cofield, and members of the media, the Lackses were understandably hesitant to trust another white person with Henrietta's story. Deborah and her siblings didn't trust Skloot's intentions and thought she was secretly working for Johns Hopkins. The only way Skloot was finally able to gain the Lackses' confidence was to treat the family as equals. She included Deborah in the research process, provided her and her siblings access to Henrietta's medical records, gave Deborah information about Elsie's death, and empowered the Lackses to take back control of Henrietta's legacy.

ARGUMENT TWO

The author then presents her second argument by explaining why being white both hurt and helped Skloot's cause as a writer: "The mere existence of *The Immortal Life of Henrietta Lacks* also demonstrates how prejudice both inhibited Skloot's progress as a journalist and worked in her favor."

On the flipside, it can be argued that it's precisely because Skloot is white that *The Immortal Life of Henrietta Lacks* was published. Unlike the Lackses, who came of age in a poor, crime-ridden, predominately black neighborhood in Baltimore, Skloot had access to more opportunities and resources. She grew up in a safe, mostly white, middle-class neighborhood in the Pacific

Northwest. As a journalist, she was privy to information from hospital staff and scientific experts, whereas the Lackses were dismissed outright. It is because of Skloot's privileged background that she was able to attend graduate school, attract a publisher, and write a book that went on to become a *New York Times* best seller, whereas Deborah couldn't get a doctor to tell her the truth about her own mother.

ARGUMENT THREE

The author completes the process of proving her thesis by using Deborah Lacks as an example of someone who rose above prejudice. "Ultimately, Skloot subverts racial stereotypes by using Deborah's progression from weak, uneducated victim to determined matriarch as one of the focal points of the book."

Ultimately, Skloot subverts racial stereotypes by using Deborah's progression from weak, uneducated victim to determined matriarch as one of the focal points of the book. In the book's first half, Deborah appears standoffish and distrustful of Skloot's motives. She has endured significant setbacks through the years. She engages in two abusive marriages; both end in divorce. She displays manic behavior, first agreeing to an interview with Skloot then deferring to her brothers' opinions. And she suffers debilitating anxiety and panic attacks for which she takes

The Morehouse School of Medicine hosts a yearly conference in Henrietta Lacks's honor. In 2015, it unveiled a bronze statue of Henrietta as her descendants watched.

medication. By the second half of the book, Deborah evolves into a woman with a strength of character to be admired. She still suffers bouts of nervousness, but she learns how to use the Internet to find out the truth about her mother's case. She faces her fears when she accompanies Skloot to the hospital where Elsie died and visits a laboratory to learn more about HeLa cells. And although she dies before she can attend, Deborah makes the decision to enroll in community college so she can better understand the science behind why HeLa cells are so important. In these actions, Deborah proves herself a strong woman who absolutely should not be dismissed because of her background or the color of her skin.

CONCLUSION

The final paragraph is the conclusion, in which the author summarizes the arguments made throughout the paper and restates her thesis using different language. In this essay, the conclusion summarizes the ways in which *The Immortal Life of Henrietta Lacks* highlights racist attitudes in medicine and in society at large. It also suggests readers might follow Skloot's example and find ways to help others fight back against racial profiling and unnecessary abuse.

For these reasons and others, *The Immortal Life of Henrietta Lacks* succeeds as a powerful polemic about an African-American family that was severely taken advantage of until a white woman brought the injustice to the world's attention. It speaks to the dangers of racism in both the scientific research and medical community and in the United States as a whole. As Skloot reminds readers, the problem didn't just exist in the pre–civil rights era. It is still widespread today. Perhaps Skloot's efforts to seek justice for Henrietta Lacks and her family will inspire others to search for similar opportunities to do the same.

THINKING CRITICALLY

Now it is your turn to assess the essay. Consider these questions:

1. Do you agree with the author's thesis? Can you think of any evidence that could disprove the author's claims?
2. What parts of the author's essay did you find most convincing? Are there any other examples you could add to this critique to strengthen the author's argument?
3. When Skloot first approached the Lacks family, they were skeptical of her intentions. Do you think she deserved this treatment? Why or why not?

OTHER APPROACHES

The previous essay was only one way to critically analyze *The Immortal Life of Henrietta Lacks*. Another paper might examine the ethical questions the book raises. Still another analysis might conduct character studies on the female protagonists in the book to compare ways in which each can be considered a feminist.

Is It Ethical?

When Henrietta Lacks's cell samples were taken before and after she died in 1951, it was not technically illegal. It also was not technically illegal for the doctors not to inform her family. In fact, according to Henrietta's care providers, their actions were excusable because she was being treated for free. The HeLa cells continue to save the lives of millions of people. But were the doctors' actions ethically and morally sound? Some companies made millions of dollars while the Lackses didn't see a dime or have health insurance. A thesis for an essay exploring these ideas might read: Despite saving millions of lives, Henrietta Lacks's doctors acted in a morally unethical way because they knowingly kept Henrietta and her family in the dark and set a precedent for future questionable practices in science.

Powerhouse Women

Many women are featured in *The Immortal Life of Henrietta Lacks*. There's Deborah Lacks, a strong mother and grandmother who shoulders the responsibility for making sure her mother's story gets told. There's Henrietta, who refuses to complain about her cancer or the pain she endures until the very end. And then there's the author, Rebecca Skloot, who takes on pharmaceutical corporations and celebrated research hospitals. Each of these women can be considered a feminist in her own way. A possible thesis arguing these ideas might be: Though male doctors took the credit for creating the world's first immortal cells, Deborah Lacks and the author Rebecca Skloot are the true history makers because of their determination to ensure Henrietta Lacks's personal legacy continues.

8

AN OVERVIEW OF *PLASTIC: A TOXIC LOVE STORY*

When author Susan Freinkel set out to research her newest book, *Plastic: A Toxic Love Story*, she began by making a list of every piece of plastic she touched in the course of a day. Alarm clock. Refrigerator handle. Bottle of dish soap. Bag of frozen strawberries. By the time 24 hours had passed, the list was four pages long, totaling 196 items. The next day, she recorded all the items that weren't made out of plastic. Toilet paper. Cotton bed sheets. Wood floor. Doorknob. This

Plastics are found everywhere on the planet, from our kitchens to our beaches.

list contained 102 items. She was surrounded by nearly twice as many plastic items as nonplastic ones.[1]

So, what *is* plastic? Freinkel asked herself. What is it made of? Do we take in materials that are harmful to our bodies when we drink out of a plastic water bottle? Where does plastic go when it gets recycled, and how does that process work exactly? Freinkel attempts to answer these questions and more in her book. She does so by traveling to plastic manufacturing plants and recycling centers around the world and by profiling eight familiar objects many people have been exposed to at one point in their lives: a comb, a chair, a Frisbee, an intravenous (IV) bag, a disposable lighter, a grocery bag, a soda bottle, and a credit card.

Origins

Freinkel's first step was to look back into plastic's origins. The word *plastic* stems from the Greek verb *plassein*, which means "to mold or shape."[2] According to Freinkel, there are tens of thousands of types of plastic.[3] Most are composed of elements such as hydrogen, carbon, oxygen, nitrogen, and chlorine combined to form molecules. They are created from chemicals found in oil, natural gas, coal, or even plants. Though each type of plastic has a different purpose, they all have one thing in common: they are polymers, substances that are made up of a chain of very large molecules, which, in turn, contain many smaller molecules called monomers.

One of the earliest types of plastic was celluloid. Invented in 1869, celluloid was created to mimic materials found in nature. It consists of a mixture of nitric acid and the organic compound found in cotton called cellulose. Celluloid was later used to make everything from filmstrips to toothbrush handles to combs.

The introduction of celluloid into product development came about at the perfect time, Freinkel discovered in her research. No longer reliant on dwindling or expensive natural resources such as wood or ivory, manufacturers could churn out more products that lasted longer for a consumption-obsessed middle class. By the time industrial manufacturing was in full swing in the early 1940s, celluloid was so popular the military started using it to create parachutes, helmet liners, and aircraft parts. It was a great replacement for rubber, which was scarce during the war. From 1939 to 1945, plastic production mushroomed from

213 pounds (97 kg) per year to 818 million pounds (371 million kg).[4]

A Hot Material

Freinkel next set out to explore how the material affects society. It soon became clear that plastic was a mixed blessing. In the years following World War II, it seemed to be everywhere and was improving Americans' lives in many ways. Necessary items such as toothbrushes, cooking utensils, and household containers could be mass-produced and were therefore readily available to the public and for export around the world. In addition, because plastic is so flexible, it can be formed into almost any product, from furniture to car parts.

Another industry that ballooned in the years following World War II was toy manufacturing. Between 1940 and 1960, toy sales soared from $84 million to $1.25 billion.[5] A majority of those toys—Frisbees, Barbie dolls, Silly Putty, toy soldiers, and farm animals—were constructed out of plastic.

By the second half of the 1900s, plastic manufacturers were making Americans' lives even easier and more comfortable with products that were designed to save time. Styrofoam used for flotation devices by

The first Barbie doll came out in 1959

the Coast Guard during World War II became the perfect material for disposable plates and cups that didn't need to be washed. Plastic wrap used to secure cargo on US military ships could now be used to protect leftover food in the fridge. Waterproof plastic bags could transport groceries home from the market in the rain.

Life magazine named this new era at its dawn with its 1955 headline: "Throwaway Living."[6]

Plastic made Americans' lives safer in certain ways during this time, too, especially in the field of medicine. Single-use plastic gloves, syringes, and plastic packages of bandages were already sterilized. These timesaving items meant doctors could treat more patients. Premature babies had a much higher survival rate after neonatal intensive care units started placing them inside protective plastic incubators just after birth. Blood or saline delivered to patients through plastic tubing and IV bags rather than breakable glass vials made blood transfusions or IV-drug treatment for sick patients virtually catastrophe- and contamination-free. In short, plastic had transformed society into a safer, more convenient place to be.

Disposable Dilemma

As Freinkel dug deeper into the effects of plastic on later generations of Americans, however, she realized plastic isn't the cure-all scientists once thought it was. In fact, once thought to be risk-free, the chemical makeup of certain plastics caused unhealthy side effects. Scientists discovered IV bags containing phthalates, chemicals used to make plastic more pliable and soft, leeched toxic residue into patients' blood. Bisphenol A (BPA), an industrial chemical used to make certain plastics such as water bottles, was shown to seep into consumers' food and, therefore, digestive systems. Studies linked increased exposure to these chemicals with an elevated risk of harmful illnesses or health problems, including heart disease, diabetes, and cancer.

The single-use phenomenon *Life* magazine once championed had its downsides, too, Freinkel discovered. Plastic takes centuries, if not millennia, to break down. Though it does photodegrade, it never disappears from the earth completely. It also has a tendency to wander. Experts estimate 1.6 billion pounds (0.7 billion kg) of plastic trash appear in the ocean each year, forming a floating garbage patch in the Pacific Ocean the size of Texas.[7]

These discarded lighters, bottle caps, and other plastic debris often end up in the stomachs of shore birds, aquatic mammals, and fish, causing widespread injury and death. In addition, bits of plastic residue make their way up the food chain and onto our dinner plates. The verdict is still out on just how harmful ingesting this toxic material might turn out to be for humans.

What to Do

Plastic: A Toxic Love Story drives home the fact that Americans' dependence on polymers isn't going away anytime soon. According to Freinkel's research, we've produced nearly as much plastic products in the last ten years as we have in all the previous decades combined.[8] She estimates if this production continues at its current rate, the world's annual plastic production levels could hit approximately 2 trillion pounds (0.9 trillion kg) by 2050.[9] Not all plastics can be recycled, and those that can must be meticulously separated and sorted into categories. The process of recycling plastic is not only complicated, it's expensive.

But there have been some positive developments. Credit card and gift card companies are working on ways to create a new type of plastic that will biodegrade when thrown into a landfill. Soda bottles made from polyethylene terephthalate (PET) can be broken down and reused to make paintbrush bristles, carpet, and even clothing. Some companies are looking into creating bottles out of polymers that are plant based rather than depending on oil or natural gas. And in 2002, a bridge 56 feet (17 m) long in New Jersey's Wharton State

Forest was constructed entirely from recycled milk jugs and plastic car bumpers.

These aren't foolproof solutions, Freinkel attests. But they're a start. "Envisioning a healthier future is one thing," she writes. "Putting new insights into practice is where the heavy lifting begins."[10]

A woman models a shirt made from recycled plastic bottles at an environmental technology show in Taiwan

9

PLASTIC IN OUR LIVES

Eco criticism is the study of literature or art as it relates to the environment. Though it gained popularity in the 1990s, eco criticism's origins extend back to the 1970s, when the modern environmental movement began. Eco critics believe a clear understanding of contemporary environmental issues is the key to understanding the work of art as a whole.

As Freinkel states in *Plastic: A Toxic Love Story*, Americans' obsession with plastic goods has increased exponentially in the last 70 years. Today, Americans consume nearly 600 billion pounds (270 billion kg) of plastic annually, more than 300 pounds (140 kg)

A man's costume draws attention to the dangers of plastic bags in the environment during an Earth Day event in San Francisco, California, in 2011.

per person.[1] Our dependence on plastic, she suggests, is real, and it's not going away anytime soon. In fact, it's growing.

But Freinkel also asks an essential question throughout her book: Can a material that is used to create so many important objects we rely on every day, from cars to takeout containers to toothbrushes to credit cards, really be bad? In profiling eight of the most common objects Americans use and documenting how they are produced, how we interact with them, and how they are thrown away, she concludes it can be. Though Freinkel presents a well-balanced analysis of how plastic has made our lives easier and better, *Plastic: A Toxic Love Story* is ultimately a persuasive discussion about the economic, ecological, and social reasons that plastic's problems may outweigh its benefits if production and consumption are left unchecked.

THESIS STATEMENT

The author begins with a short explanation of eco criticism as it relates to the content and structure of *Plastic: A Toxic Love Story*. Then she states her thesis: "Though Freinkel presents a well-balanced analysis of how plastic has made our lives easier and better, *Plastic: A Toxic Love Story* is ultimately a persuasive discussion about the economic, ecological, and social reasons that plastic's problems may outweigh its benefits if production and consumption are left unchecked." The author will demonstrate why Freinkel's book succeeds as a convincing argument against plastic dependence.

Although plastics promised "abundance on the cheap" and made mass-production of essential items such as toys and beverage bottles possible, dubious overseas labor practices and fluctuating disposal costs make plastic a socially irresponsible and economically unstable commodity.[2] Freinkel supports this theory by including personal stories and travel notes from her research. For example, the toy industry sends operations overseas to third-world countries such as China, leaving employable US workers without jobs. In turn, some overseas factories pay their workers shockingly low wages to work long hours in unsafe conditions.

ARGUMENT ONE

Next, the author begins to support her thesis by presenting the first argument: "Although plastics promised 'abundance on the cheap' and made mass-production of essential items such as toys and beverage bottles possible, dubious overseas labor practices and fluctuating disposal costs make plastic a socially irresponsible and economically unstable commodity." The author will show why outsourcing and complicated recycling practices contribute to plastic's negative image.

When researching how Frisbees are manufactured, Freinkel traveled to the Guangdong Province in China and interviewed a factory foreman. The conditions were abominable. The factory didn't have air conditioning, the pay was awful at $175 per month, and most of the workers were migrant women who slept in packed dormitories far away from their families. According to Freinkel, this is just one way plastic manufacturers try to skirt the rules to keep output high and production costs low.

Freinkel suggests that another reason excessive plastic production can become economically unsound is the complexity of recycling programs in the United States. She supports this theory with statistics. Some cities don't have recycling programs at all and many export their plastic to China to be recycled and shipped back.

Plus, because there are so many types of plastic, each has a different disposal method. Some, such as soda bottles made out of PET plastic, can be recycled and reused to make clothing. But problems arise when one type of plastic is thrown in with another type to be recycled. The foreign material can contaminate the entire batch, which is an expensive mistake. Unless recycling programs can consistently catch up, there's a good chance more plastic products will end up in the landfill. In fact, according to Freinkel's research, of 72 billion PET bottles produced in the United States each year, 55 billion are dumped due to lack of recycling programs, recycling mistakes, or human laziness.[3]

In addition to plastic manufacturers' questionable business practices, their excessive output harms the environment. Freinkel provides real-world examples and scientific explanations as evidence. Because of its synthetic makeup, most plastic doesn't biodegrade and will sit in landfills for thousands of years. But polymers do photodegrade. The ultraviolet radiation in sunlight breaks down their molecular bonds and they break apart into tiny pieces. Those pieces are still damaging because they will never fully disappear from the planet.

ARGUMENT TWO

The author then presents the second argument: "In addition to plastic manufacturers' questionable business practices, their excessive output harms the environment." She backs up this idea by discussing some of Freinkel's real-world examples of how disproportionate amounts of plastic can ruin many of the earth's increasingly fragile ecosystems

In addition, this process comes to a virtual halt in the ocean where the sun's rays only touch the surface. Using the Pacific Garbage Patch as an example, Freinkel explains why there aren't any easy solutions when it comes to dealing with the problem. A thorough sweep of the area would not only pick up plastic but also rob the area of plankton, seaweed, and fish.

ARGUMENT THREE

The author finishes proving her thesis by providing a third argument that highlights the readers' complicated role in the issue: "Perhaps Freinkel's most compelling argument for readers is the parallel she makes between plastic's negative environmental effect and Americans' laziness."

Perhaps Freinkel's most compelling argument for readers is the parallel she makes between plastic's negative environmental effect and Americans' laziness. Again, she uses statistics to support her claim. According to a US Environmental Protection Agency report, the average American generated 3.25 pounds (1.47 kg) of trash each day in 1970.[4] In 2008, that number jumped to 4.5 pounds (2 kg).[5] That's a lot of trash for the average person! It's also a sign we've become more dependent on a lifestyle that enables us to use plastic plates, cups, and shampoo bottles once, then throw them away without thinking about the consequences.

Freinkel brings up another important point: Americans' complicated relationship with recycling. Though some cities such as Portland, Oregon; and San Francisco, California; have curbside recycling programs that include most plastics and compost, others don't. Instead of figuring out which items can and cannot be recycled and driving to the closest recycling center, many people throw their plastic items in the trash. Plus, because the burden and financial responsibility of recycling is placed on the consumer instead of the manufacturer, there's no incentive for companies

A small sample of garbage collected on a research expedition to the Pacific Garbage Patch

to make products that will last longer or contain ingredients that can be recycled more easily.

In *Plastic: A Toxic Love Story*, Freinkel documents many of the ways plastic is ruining our Earth. But she also offers a silver lining in the form of possible solutions that might inspire future change. Companies are researching ways to create biodegradable credit cards. States such as Michigan have implemented a bottle bill law, under which stores are given incentives to recycle their PET bottles and customers are given ten cents for every plastic bottle they bring back to the store. And there's the bridge in New Jersey made entirely out of recycled milk cartons and plastic car parts. Freinkel's book proves just how complicated our dependence on plastic can be. And she leaves us with a warning: "If we want to bring about a greener world, personal virtue must take into account the larger political and social contexts of individual actions."[6]

CONCLUSION

The final paragraph is the conclusion, in which the author summarizes the arguments made throughout the paper and restates her thesis using different language. In this essay, the conclusion reiterates plastic's negative effect on the environment. But, like Freinkel's multisided book, the final paragraph also presents examples of how companies and individuals are doing their part to use plastic in positive and responsible ways.

THINKING CRITICALLY

Now it is your turn to assess the essay. Consider these questions:

1. Do you agree with the author's thesis? Can you think of any evidence that could disprove the author's claims?
2. What parts of the author's argument did you find most convincing? Is there any evidence you could add to this critique to strengthen the author's argument?
3. The author suggests that Americans' laziness contributes to the world's dependence on plastic. Can you think of real-world examples that either prove or disprove this statement? How can you do your part to make the world less dependent on plastic?

OTHER APPROACHES

The previous essay was only one way to critically analyze *Plastic: A Toxic Love Story*. A different paper might take the opposite approach, arguing why the benefits of plastic far outweigh its negative qualities. Yet another essay might discuss how the presence of more and more plastic in the world reflects parallel social and cultural moments throughout history.

The Pros of Plastic

Most plastic won't biodegrade. Some types aren't even recyclable. But there are arguably benefits to its existence. Products made out of plastic are built to last; they will be around for generations. Many plastic objects don't melt in the heat. Plus, some plastic can be recycled into other usable objects such as clothing, carpet, and furniture upholstery. Some experts might say that plastics' positive qualities outweigh its detriments. A thesis for an essay exploring these ideas might read: Although Freinkel provides evidence of the problems with plastic, her book also shows how plastic can be considered the first "green" consumer product because of its durability and versatility.

History Speaks

Prior to World War II, Americans relied on objects that were sturdy and could be reused. As a popular Depression era expression so aptly put it: "Use it up, wear it out, make it do, or do without."[7] But after the war was over and supplies became more abundant, plastic became more popular. In the 1950s, when disposable items signified a life of ease and comfort, plastic sales shot through the roof. It's only since the 1970s when the environmental movement picked up steam that dependence on plastic has become a pressing issue. A possible thesis statement arguing these ideas might be: In *Plastic: A Toxic Love Story*, the rise of plastic and its increased popularity can be directly linked to cultural and social movements throughout history.

ANALYZE IT!

Now that you have learned different approaches to analyzing a work, are you ready to perform your own analysis? You have read that this type of evaluation can help you look at literature in a new way and make you pay attention to certain issues you may not have otherwise recognized. So, why not use one of these approaches to consider a fresh take on your favorite work?

First, choose a philosophy, critical theory, or other approach and consider which work or works you want to analyze. Remember the approach you choose is a springboard for asking questions about the works.

Next, write a specific question that relates to your approach or philosophy. Then you can form your thesis, which should provide the answer to that question. Your thesis is the most important part of your analysis and offers an argument about the work, considering its characters, plot, or literary techniques, or what it says about society or the world. Recall that the thesis statement typically appears at the very end of the introductory paragraph of your essay. It is usually only one sentence long.

After you have written your thesis, find evidence to back it up. Good places to start are in the work itself or in journals or articles that discuss what other people have said about it. You may also want to read about the author or creator's life so you can get a sense of what factors may have affected the creative process. This can be especially useful if you are considering how the work connects to history or the author's intent.

You should also explore parts of the book that seem to disprove your thesis and create an argument against them. As you do this, you might want to address what others have written about the book. Their quotes may help support your claim.

Before you start analyzing a work, think about the different arguments made in this book. Reflect on how evidence supporting the thesis was presented. Did you find that some of the techniques used to back up the arguments were more convincing than others? Try these methods as you prove your thesis in your own analysis paper.

When you are finished writing your analysis, read it over carefully. Is your thesis statement understandable? Do the supporting arguments flow logically, with the topic of each paragraph clearly stated? Can you add any information that would present your readers with a stronger argument in favor of your thesis? Were you able to use quotes from the book, as well as from other critics, to enhance your ideas?

Did you see the work in a new light?

GLOSSARY

BIGOTED
Intolerant of another person's race, ethnicity, or religion.

BIODEGRADE
To break down or decompose by bacteria or other living things.

COMMUNIST
A person who believes in communism, an economic system based on the elimination of private ownership of factories, land, and other means of economic production.

COUP
An attempt to overthrow leaders.

DENOUEMENT
The final section of a book, play, or movie in which different parts of the plot come together and matters are explained or resolved.

JEHOVAH'S WITNESS
A member of a religious group that believes in the imminent destruction of the world's wickedness and that seeks to evangelize to others.

MEMOIR
A type of nonfiction that tells a true story about a period in its author's life from his or her perspective.

OMNISCIENT
All knowing.

POLEMIC
A strong attack against someone else's beliefs or opinions.

PREJUDICE

An unfair feeling of dislike for a person or group because of race, sex, or religion.

PROGRESSIVE

Advanced; in favor of liberal ideas or social reform for positive change.

RACISM

Poor treatment of or violence against people because of their race.

RECYCLING

Converting plastic and other wastes into reusable materials.

SCOURGE

Something that causes a lot of suffering or trouble.

SEGREGATION

The practice of separating groups of people based on race, gender, ethnicity, or other factors.

STEREOTYPE

An often unfair and untrue belief that many people have about all people or things with a particular characteristic—for example, gender or race.

SUBVERT

To overturn a thing or idea on its head.

SYNTHETIC

Something made by humans.

XENOPHOBIC

Exhibiting a dislike, distrust, or fear of people from other countries.

ADDITIONAL
RESOURCES

SELECTED BIBLIOGRAPHY

Engle, Margarita. *Enchanted Air*. New York: Atheneum, 2015. Print.

Freinkel, Susan. *Plastic: A Toxic Love Story*. Boston, MA: Houghton, 2011. Print.

Skloot, Rebecca. *The Immortal Life of Henrietta Lacks*. New York: Crown, 2010. Print.

Swanson, James L. *Chasing Lincoln's Killer*. New York: Scholastic, 2009. Print.

Woodson, Jacqueline. *Brown Girl Dreaming*. New York: Nancy Paulsen, 2014. Print.

FURTHER READINGS

Capek, Michael. *Civil Rights Movement*. Minneapolis: Abdo, 2014. Print.

EarthWorks Group. *The New 50 Simple Things Kids Can Do to Save the Earth*. Kansas City, MO: Andrews McMeel, 2009. Print.

Engle, Margarita. *The Surrender Tree: Poems of Cuba's Struggle for Freedom*. New York: Square Fish, 2010. Print.

Forman, Lillian. *Stem Cell Research*. Minneapolis: Abdo, 2008. Print.

Harris, Laurie Lanzen. *How to Analyze the Works of Abraham Lincoln*. Minneapolis: Abdo, 2013. Print.

WEBSITES

To learn more about Essential Literary Genres, visit **booklinks.abdopublishing.com**. These links are routinely monitored and updated to provide the most current information available.

FOR MORE INFORMATION

For more information on this subject, contact or visit the following organizations:

Ford's Theatre Museum and Center for Education and Leadership
511 Tenth Street, NW
Washington, DC 20004
202-347-4833
http://www.fords.org/
The Ford's Theatre Museum and Center for Education and Leadership offers interactive exhibits, artifacts, and programs related to Abraham Lincoln's presidency, assassination, and legacy.

The Museum of Science and Industry
5700 S Lake Shore Drive
Chicago, IL 60637
773-684-1414
http://www.msichicago.org/
The largest science museum in the Western Hemisphere, the Museum of Science and Industry specializes in all sorts of interactive exhibits, including "It's a Material World," where visitors learn the history and science behind the objects they use every day.

National Civil Rights Museum
450 Mulberry Street
Memphis, TN 38103
901-521-9699
http://civilrightsmuseum.org/
This museum walks visitors through civil rights history into race issues of today. Rotating exhibits on the Black Panthers, the Freedom Rides of 1961, sit-ins, and more are on display.

SOURCE NOTES

CHAPTER 1. INTRODUCTION TO LITERARY GENRES

None.

CHAPTER 2. OVERVIEWS OF *ENCHANTED AIR* AND *BROWN GIRL DREAMING*

1. Margarita Engle. *Enchanted Air*. New York: Atheneum, 2015. Print. 7.
2. Ibid. 9.
3. Ibid. 9.
4. Ibid. 11.
5. Jacqueline Woodson. *Brown Girl Dreaming*. New York: Nancy Paulson, 2014. Print. 2.

CHAPTER 3. A CHANGING SOCIETY

1. Jacqueline Woodson. *Brown Girl Dreaming*. New York: Nancy Paulson, 2014. Print. 1.
2. Ibid. 2.
3. Ibid. 237.
4. Ibid. 73.

CHAPTER 4. AN OVERVIEW OF *CHASING LINCOLN'S KILLER*

1. James L. Swanson. *Chasing Lincoln's Killer*. New York: Scholastic, 2009. Print. 1–2.
2. "If Slavery Is Not Wrong, Nothing Is Wrong: Abraham Lincoln to A. G. Hodges." *American Treasures of the Library of Congress*. Library of Congress, 27 July 2010. Web. 5 July 2016.
3. James L. Swanson. *Chasing Lincoln's Killer*. New York: Scholastic, 2009. Print. Intro.
4. Ibid. 43.
5. Ibid. 45.

CHAPTER 5. LITERARY ELEMENTS IN NARRATIVE NONFICTION

1. James L. Swanson. *Chasing Lincoln's Killer*. New York: Scholastic, 2009. Print. 127.
2. Ibid. 10.
3. Ibid. 20.

CHAPTER 6. AN OVERVIEW OF *THE IMMORTAL LIFE OF HENRIETTA LACKS*

1. Rebecca Skloot. *The Immortal Life of Henrietta Lacks.* New York: Crown, 2010. Print. 4.
2. Ibid. 14.
3. Ibid. 41.
4. Ibid. 96.
5. Ibid. 164.

CHAPTER 7. DISCRIMINATION IN MEDICINE

1. Rebecca Skloot. *The Immortal Life of Henrietta Lacks.* New York: Crown, 2010. Print. 15.
2. Ibid. 29–30.

CHAPTER 8. AN OVERVIEW OF *PLASTIC: A TOXIC LOVE STORY*

1. Susan Freinkel. *Plastic: A Toxic Love Story.* Boston, MA: Houghton, 2011. Print. 2–3.
2. Ibid. 14.
3. Ibid. 4.
4. Ibid. 25.
5. Ibid. 56.
6. Ben Cosgrove. "'Throwaway Living': When Tossing Out Everything Was All the Rage." *Time.* Time, 15 May 2014. Web. 5 July 2016.
7. Susan Freinkel. *Plastic: A Toxic Love Story.* Boston, MA: Houghton, 2011. Print. 119, 129.
8. Ibid. 232.
9. Ibid. 232.
10. Ibid. 202.

CHAPTER 9. PLASTIC IN OUR LIVES

1. Susan Freinkel. *Plastic: A Toxic Love Story.* Boston, MA: Houghton, 2011. Print. 7.
2. Ibid. 7.
3. Ibid. 175.
4. Ibid. 194.
5. Ibid. 194.
6. Ibid. 229.
7. Ibid. 121.

INDEX

ABOUT THE AUTHOR

Alexis Burling has written dozens of articles and books for young readers on a variety of topics including current events, famous people, nutrition and fitness, relationships, and cooking. Her reviews of both adult and young adult books, author interviews, and other publishing industry–related articles have been published in the *New York Times*, the *Washington Post*, and the *San Francisco Chronicle*.